Jack-o-Lanterns

by Lola M. Schaefer

Consulting Editor:
Gail Saunders-Smith, Ph.D.

Consultant:
Terry Kuseske
National Council for
the Social Studies

Pebble Books

an imprint of Capstone Press
Mankato, Minnesota

1

Pebble Books are published by Capstone Press
818 North Willow Street, Mankato, Minnesota 56001
http://www.capstone-press.com

Library of Congress Cataloging-in-Publication Data
Schaefer, Lola M., 1950–
　　Jack-o-lanterns/by Lola M. Schaefer.
　　p. cm.—(Fall fun)
　　Includes bibliographical references and index.
　　Summary: Simple text and photographs present the features of jack-o-lanterns
and the different kinds of faces that they can have.
　　ISBN 0-7368-0105-7
　　1. Halloween decorations—Juvenile literature. 2. Jack-o-lanterns—Juvenile
literature. [1. Jack-o-lanterns. 2. Halloween decorations. 3. Handicraft.] I. Title.
II. Series: Schaefer, Lola M. 1950–　Fall fun.
TT900.H32S33　1999
745.594′1—dc21

98-7346
CIP
AC

Note to Parents and Teachers

This series supports units on fall celebrations. This book describes and illustrates the features and expressions of jack-o-lanterns. The photographs support emergent readers in understanding the text. Repetition of words and phrases helps emergent readers learn new words. This book introduces emergent readers to vocabulary used in this subject area. The vocabulary is defined in the Words to Know section. Emergent readers may need assistance in reading some words and in using the Table of Contents, Words to Know, Read More, Internet Sites, and Index/Word List sections of the book.

2

Table of Contents

A jack-o-lantern has
two eyes.

A jack-o-lantern has
a nose.

A jack-o-lantern has
a mouth.

Two eyes, a nose, and a mouth make a face.

Some faces are happy.

Some faces are sad.

Some faces are scary.

Some faces are funny.

Jack-o-lantern faces glow with yellow light.

Words to Know

glow—to give off a low, even light

jack-o-lantern—a pumpkin with a face cut into it; people take out the insides and put a light in the pumpkin.

scary—causing fright

Read More

Hall, Zoe. *It's Pumpkin Time.* New York: Scholastic, 1994.

Palmer, Ed. *Pumpkin Carving.* New York: Sterling Publishing, 1995.

Widmann, Emily. *Pumpkin Cut-Ups: Super Patterns for Carving Perfect Pumpkins.* New York: Scholastic, 1992.

Internet Sites

Halloween Hollow
http://www.bconnex.net/~mbuchana/realms/halloween/index.html

Halloween Music and Fingerplays
http://members.aol.com/aactchrday/music/halloween.html

Pumpkin Carving
http://www.hauntedhome.com/theHouse/Pumpkin/index.htm

Index/Word List

are, 13, 15, 17, 19
eyes, 5, 11
face, 11, 13, 15, 17,
  19, 21
funny, 19
glow, 21
happy, 13
has, 5, 7, 9
jack-o-lantern, 5, 7,
  9, 21

light, 21
make, 11
mouth, 9, 11
nose, 7, 11
sad, 15
scary, 17
some, 13, 15, 17, 19
two, 5, 11
yellow, 21

Word Count: 47
Early-Intervention Level: 4

Editorial Credits
Martha Hillman, editor; Clay Schotzko/Icon Productions, cover designer;
  Sheri Gosewisch, photo researcher

Photo Credits
Barbara Comnes, 8
Cheryl A. Ertelt, 6
Chuck Place, cover
Photobank/Kent Knudson, 12
Unicorn Stock Photos/David P. Dill, 1; Bets Anderson Bailly, 10; Robert W. Ginn, 16;
Rod Furgason, 18; Royce L. Bair, 20
Visuals Unlimited/D. Cavagnaro, 4; Mark E. Gibson, 14